the little book of
MINDFULNESS

gilly pickup

summersdale

THE LITTLE BOOK OF MINDFULNESS

An Hachette UK Company
www.hachette.co.uk

Summersdale Publishers Ltd
Part of Octopus Publishing Group Limited
Carmelite House
50 Victoria Embankment
LONDON
EC4Y 0DZ
UK

www.summersdale.com

Printed and bound in the Czech Republic

ISBN: 978-1-78685-967-9

Substantial discounts on bulk quantities of Summersdale books are available to corporations, professional associations and other organizations. For details contact general enquiries: telephone: +44 (0) 1243 771107 or email: enquiries@summersdale.com.

INTRODUCTION

Welcome to *The Little Book of Mindfulness*.

You may have chosen this book because you want to feel less stressed, improve your quality of life or increase your focus. Whatever your motive, there is no doubt that practising mindfulness is one of the easiest and most effective solutions to improving your life in many areas.

Full of tips, advice and thoughtful quotes to help you embrace the power of the present moment, this book delivers all you need to make every day one of appreciation and peace. Happy reading!

Do not **dwell**
in the past, do not
dream of the **future**,
concentrate the mind on
the **present** moment.

Buddhist proverb

THE PRESENT MOMENT IS FILLED WITH JOY AND HAPPINESS. IF YOU ARE ATTENTIVE, YOU WILL SEE IT.

Thích Nhất Hạnh

MINDFULNESS EXPLAINED

What exactly is mindfulness? Also known as present moment awareness, in simple terms mindfulness is about focusing on the present moment. It is the practice of being fully aware of where you are and what you are doing, without becoming overwhelmed by everything that is happening around you. This is achieved by being totally conscious of your surroundings, emotions and thoughts, while concentrating your attention on whatever is happening in the here and now.

You might ask yourself, how will mindfulness benefit me? For one thing, it can help banish those niggling feelings of anxiety and tension that sometimes come along and threaten your peace of mind. Living mindfully brings many other rewards, including improved mood and strengthened mental health; these are covered in this book.

Mindfulness isn't difficult, we just need to remember to do it.

Sharon Salzberg

It's **good** to have an end in **mind**, but in the end what counts is how you **travel**.

Orna Ross

NO DISTRACTIONS

When you first start to practise mindfulness, eliminate distractions. Choose a peaceful space, switch off your phone and cut out as much external noise as possible. Focus on your breathing. Notice how each breath moves in and out of your body. If your mind starts to wander, bring your focus back to your breathing. The more you focus, the easier it gets – trust me!

If you notice that you're thinking ahead to what you're going to do next, gently nudge your attention back to the present. Although mindfulness is all about paying attention to what's happening around you right now, it doesn't mean shutting out every thought you have. Your mind doesn't come with an "off" switch. It is about dealing more creatively with those thoughts and experiencing life as it unfolds, moment by moment.

The point of mindfulness
is not to get rid of
thought but to learn to
use thought skilfully.

Jack Kornfield

ANYONE CAN DO IT

Anyone can practise mindfulness. It doesn't matter about your background or education, or how old you are. You don't need a guru or to be religious to benefit from mindful practice. Simply go at your own pace and don't worry about how long it takes to "get the hang of it"; like any skill, mindfulness requires practice to achieve satisfying results. Mindfulness requires no equipment, no qualifications and just a little perseverance, and with practice you too will reap the benefits.

ANYTIME, ANYWHERE

One of the great things about mindfulness is that you can practise it wherever you are. You don't even need to set aside a special time because you can be mindful of your surroundings at any moment in your day. While out walking, for example, or when you are in the gym; making dinner or relaxing. All you have to do is focus your attention on your body, thoughts, emotions or the surrounding environment.

Of course, developing daily mind-fulness practice takes patience and determination. It can be hard work to keep pulling your mind back to the present moment. One of the easiest ways to do this is to breathe slowly and deeply. Stay with it. As you become more familiar with the practice, benefits will become more obvious. You will start to feel more present, peaceful and alive. Remember, mindfulness works like a muscle: the more you exercise it, the stronger it gets.

SOMETIMES THE MOST IMPORTANT THING IN A WHOLE DAY IS THE REST WE TAKE BETWEEN TWO DEEP BREATHS.

Etty Hillesum

You must live in the present, launch yourself on every wave, find your eternity in each moment.

Henry David Thoreau

DAILY ROUTINES

Pick a routine daily activity that you normally do on autopilot and make it mindful. Let's say brushing your teeth, for instance, or getting dressed. Many of us do these activities barely noticing what we are doing. Pay attention to squeezing the toothpaste onto the brush, the contours of your mouth, what the toothpaste tastes like and how the brush feels against each tooth. Think about the clothes you put on. Are the colours muted or bright? Is the fabric soft or textured? How do the clothes make you feel?

Take the opportunity to consider how you feel throughout the experience. When you pay close attention, you may pick up on things you haven't noticed or thought about before and you will find more enjoyment in these seemingly simple or mundane tasks. In a nutshell, whatever you're doing, be aware of it and take it all in.

The past is behind,
learn from it. The
future is ahead, prepare
for it. The present
is here, live it.

Thomas S. Monson

FOCUS ON THE HERE AND NOW

Don't compare the past with the present. If you find your mind is drifting while you are having a mindful moment, make your thoughts home in on what's good now by thinking of one thing that you are grateful for. It needn't be anything huge, it could simply be you are grateful that the sun is shining or appreciating your morning cup of tea or coffee.

Mindfulness
can help people
of **any age**. That's
because we become
what we **think**.

Goldie Hawn

YOU'VE BEEN
ASLEEP FOR
A LONG TIME.
ISN'T IT TIME
TO AWAKEN?

Ajahn Chah

UNDERSTAND YOURSELF

Mindfulness enables you to be more aware of your body and is the key to understanding yourself. Mindfulness means being focused on your actions, which helps you to act with purpose. When you act with purpose your thought processes become clearer to you.

Knowing yourself
is the beginning
of all wisdom.

Aristotle

When you have the
constant focus of going
within and then acting,
your life will unfold
in magical ways.

Elizabeth Jo

FEELING BETTER

Those who practise mindfulness experience greater feelings of well-being. Research shows that mindfulness can improve physical health too by helping to reduce high blood pressure and chronic pain. It also increases your ability to handle stressful situations as well as enhancing quality of sleep, enabling you to enjoy a deeper, more peaceful slumber.

Awareness is
the greatest agent
for **change**.

Eckhart Tolle

LIFE IS REALLY SIMPLE, BUT WE INSIST ON MAKING IT COMPLICATED.

Confucius

RISE AND SHINE

When you wake up in the morning, don't just jump out of bed to start the day, take time to be conscious of your body. Become aware of your thoughts, observe them as they come and go, letting them pass like clouds in the sky. Focus on your breathing. Listen to sounds around you and stretch your whole body to awaken your muscles. Make your bed mindfully to create a calm transition from sleep to the day ahead. When brushing your hair, notice every detail.

It's also important to find a few minutes in your morning routine to sit calmly instead of rushing to start the day's activities. Focus on your breathing and visualize each breath filling your body with golden light. You will feel energized and ready for the new day.

Put your heart, mind, intellect and soul even to your smallest acts. This is the secret of success.

Swami Sivananda

THE PRESENT MOMENT IS ALL WE HAVE

Mindfulness helps nurture awareness by paying attention to the present. Our minds have a habit of wandering away when we leave them to their own devices. If you notice that your thoughts are drifting, bring them back by noting what you are seeing, hearing, touching, smelling and tasting. The best way to move past intrusive thoughts is to acknowledge them and then gently release them, turning your mind back to the present.

Mindfulness is the open-hearted **energy** of being aware in the **present** moment. It's the daily **cultivation** of touching life **deeply**.

Laurie Buchanan

THE BEST WAY TO CAPTURE MOMENTS IS TO PAY ATTENTION. THIS IS HOW WE CULTIVATE MINDFULNESS.

Jon Kabat-Zinn

WALK MINDFULLY

With daily practice, any activity you do can become a mindful activity. Take walking to the shops or to work, for example. As you walk, be aware of everything around you by engaging your five senses. Take deep breaths, listen to the sound of your footsteps, be aware of your body. We all tend to rush from one place to another; walking mindfully is your chance to slow down, appreciate your surroundings, let a feeling of calm wash over you. Allow yourself extra time to get to wherever it is you are going so that you don't feel the need to rush.

If you are out in the countryside, take notice of the blooming wildflowers and leaves on the trees, the sound of birdsong, the sight of animals grazing in the fields. If you are walking in a city, be aware of the aroma of coffee as you pass coffee shops, how doors feel if you go into a shop – are they made of wood, metal or glass? Notice the details – chimneys, rooftops, windows, architecture. Really look and see everything. You'll be surprised at how much you missed before!

You're only here for
a short visit. Don't
hurry, don't worry.

Walter Hagen

Joy is everywhere.
It is in the earth's
green covering of
grass; in the blue
serenity of the sky.

Rabindranath Tagore

SLOW DOWN, DON'T HURRY

These days life demands so much of us, it's really no wonder it often feels as though we are continually racing against the clock. Slow down by taking a deep breath, hold it for the count of three, then slowly release it. Focus on each of your senses, one by one, breathing deeply as you do so to promote a sense of calm.

We too should make
ourselves empty, that
the great soul of the
universe may fill us
with its breath.

Laurence Binyon

Our life is **frittered** away by detail...
simplify, simplify.

Henry David Thoreau

DAILY PLEASURE

It is all too easy to let time pass without being particularly aware of it. An important part of mindfulness practice is to remember to feel joy every day and regard each day as your favourite. Notice the little pleasures – be mindful of the wind in your hair, how the sun feels on your skin, the fresh scent of newly laundered clothes or the sweetness of a fresh strawberry on your tongue.

ALL ABOUT APPRECIATION

We're often so engrossed in our thoughts that we don't pause to appreciate our surroundings. This means interesting details are often overlooked. Encourage yourself to take note of the oft-ignored: you may usually notice how a meal tastes but appreciate how enticing it looks, its colour palette or the charred and crispy textures.

Your food is a good place to practise mindfulness because it engages all of your senses. You could dedicate one day a week to focusing on just one sense while eating. For example, on Monday you could listen for the sound of your food while cooking, how it sizzles and pops, and how it crunches in your mouth. On Tuesday you could note the feel of your food, how the cool, hard vegetables become warm and soft as they cook. Really see the things you take for granted every day.

DINNER DATE

Set aside time to eat your evening meal. Make this a part of your day where you can refocus and reconnect with yourself. Eat slowly, savouring the taste of the food. Put your knife and fork down between each mouthful. Give the food your full attention, being grateful for the meal you are eating. Don't multitask by watching television, checking social media or chatting with friends online.

Prepare your meals with love and focus. Notice the tantalizing textures of the ingredients at your fingertips. When you sit down to eat make yourself engage in the experience by appreciating the smells, tastes and textures of the food. Focus your attention on the act of eating. Your meals will taste better and you will feel better for it.

Be present in all
things and **thankful**
for all things.

Maya Angelou

YOU MUST FIND THE PLACE INSIDE YOURSELF WHERE NOTHING IS IMPOSSIBLE.

Deepak Chopra

WHEN YOU EAT

At mealtimes sit with your feet planted firmly on the floor and straighten your spine to maximize room for breathing. Before you start to eat you could light a candle and put it on the table to help encourage feelings of calmness and serenity. If you are one of those people who eats too quickly, you could even set a timer for 20 minutes to make sure you don't bolt your food.

To help get the most from each mealtime, remember to eat at a steady pace. Relish every bite and chew slowly to bring your awareness to every taste sensation. Engage your senses of sight, sound, smell, touch and taste. Research shows that people who take their time eating tend to fill up quicker and feel full for longer.

When walking, walk.
When eating, eat.

Zen proverb

DON'T BELIEVE EVERYTHING YOU THINK. THOUGHTS ARE JUST THAT – THOUGHTS.

Allan Lokos

NO TIME LIKE THE PRESENT

The past is gone and the future hasn't arrived yet. You can't change what has happened and you don't know what will come. Stop mulling over past or future tasks and bring yourself back to the here and now. The present is the place of power. Now, in this moment, you can choose to be happy.

All our dreams can come true, if we have the courage to pursue them.

Walt Disney

TAKE IT SLOWLY

It's easy to try to cram as much as possible into the day. When you feel overwhelmed, reduce the number of things on your to-do list. Set aside blocks of time when you will complete your tasks and turn your electronic devices off, so you won't be interrupted or feel tempted to distract yourself by checking your social media. Work slowly, carefully and deliberately on one task at a time. Keep your mind on the present and focus on your actions.

Take the time to enjoy whatever it is you are doing. You may notice that you find completing errands and life admin relaxing and fulfilling when you're not rushing to get them finished. When you perform tasks more slowly, you are being more thorough and you'll avoid feeling stressed.

For fast-acting **relief**,
try **slowing** down.

Lily Tomlin

Everything you do can
be done better from a
place of relaxation.

Stephen C. Paul

GREETINGS

The Sanskrit greeting "namaste" translates as "I bow to you". To perform namaste, place your hands together over your heart (at the heart chakra), close your eyes and slightly bow your head. Keep the phrase and its meaning in mind when meeting other people. It will remind you to listen mindfully and look for the light in their words and actions.

It's important to be
thoughtful and mindful
about the things you
say to other people.

Evan Spiegel

Quiet the mind and the soul will **speak**.

Ma Jaya Sati Bhagavati

WHEREVER YOU ARE, BE ALL THERE.

Jim Elliot

THE MUSIC OF MINDFULNESS

Listening to music is a good mindfulness exercise. Choose something soothing and begin by turning off all devices but the one playing music. Sit in a comfortable position in a space where you can minimize any outer distractions. Spend a few moments resting, your attention on your breathing, immersing yourself in inhaling and exhaling.

As you begin to listen to the music, focus on each note. Really take notice of the instruments, the dynamics and the pacing. Notice any feelings that the music conjures up for you and any sensations that occur in your body. If other thoughts creep into your head, gently bring your attention back to the music. Afterward, notice how much calmer you feel.

Why not just live in the moment, especially if it has a good beat?

Goldie Hawn

Make **yourself** a priority once in a while. It's not **selfish**. It's **necessary**.

Karen A. Baquiran

BE GRATEFUL

There is always something to appreciate in life. Mindfulness encourages us to embrace acceptance and gratitude, which in turn allows us to appreciate what we already have. This makes us feel happier and our life becomes more satisfying. Changing our mindset reduces negative thought processes and enables us to appreciate the good in our lives.

When you realize there
is nothing lacking,
the whole world
belongs to you.

Lao Tzu

LISTEN TO
THE SILENCE

Close your eyes and listen for a minute to the sounds around you. Don't do anything else except listen. Being comfortable with silence is essential to mindfulness practice. Become aware of your thoughts. Focus on your breathing. Be at one with the silence and stillness. It will bring peace.

Let us be silent, that
we may hear the
whispers of the gods.

Ralph Waldo Emerson

HEAR OTHERS SPEAK

Sometimes we do not truly listen to the people we are talking to. We may be considering what we are going to say in reply, or perhaps we are thinking of our own opinions on the subject. We often speak without waiting for the other person to finish. Next time you start an interesting conversation with a friend or loved one, try listening mindfully.

Focus on really hearing what that person is saying. Look at them as they talk. Listen to the person's words without judgement or the need to immediately express a view. When you are not being mindful, you can easily be distracted by your own thoughts and don't concentrate on what the other person is saying. And here's something to ponder over: the word "listen" is an anagram of "silent". Wait until the other person has finished talking before you speak.

BE PASSIONATE ABOUT EVERYONE AND EVERYTHING THAT ENTERS YOUR LIFE.

Wayne W. Dyer

The greatest
communication
is usually how we are
rather than what we say.

Joseph Goldstein

With mindfulness there
is more to unlearn
than there is to learn.

Michael H. Brooks

ENERGY BOOST!

Regardless of how many things you have to do, stop between tasks and breathe three complete breaths – this gives you an energy recharge to carry on with your day. Remember to allow yourself plenty of rest, too, especially when there are likely to be extra demands on your time.

TO BE CREATIVE MEANS TO BE IN LOVE WITH LIFE.

Osho

Your **mind** is your instrument. **Learn** to be its **master** and not its slave.

Remez Sasson

WASH AWAY YOUR CARES

Next time you have a shower or take a bath, be mindful of all your senses. See the water as it flows from the taps, take notice of how the warm water feels against your skin and enjoy the scent of the soap or shower gel. Listen to the patter of water at your feet or the splashing as you clean yourself. Wash all your cares away.

You could make your shower or bath time something special by playing some relaxing music and using scented candles. Also soothing to the senses are aromatherapy oils, such as lavender, jasmine, sandalwood and ylang-ylang. You could add some to the water or put drops on a cotton wool ball or tissue and place in a bowl nearby. Breathe in the aromas around you. Really enjoy the experience. When you're finished, wrap yourself up in cosy, fluffy towels.

Nothing is worth
more than this day.

Johann Wolfgang von Goethe

THOUGHTS ARE ONLY THOUGHTS – NO MORE

Remember that thoughts are just that – they are thoughts; they don't automatically represent reality. You can and should observe them without being subject to them. When you practise mindfulness you will find you can enjoy the fullness of the moment, instead of focusing part of your attention on the past or the future.

After all, the best thing
one can do when it's
raining is to let it rain.

Henry Wadsworth Longfellow

WONDERS OF WILDLIFE

Nature inspires. Its beauty and complexity has powerful appeal. When you're out in the country or on a train journey, look out for cows and sheep grazing in the fields or perhaps deer on the moorlands. In parks or gardens notice squirrels scampering across the ground, dashing up tree trunks, leaping from branch to branch. See how butterflies flit from flower to flower. Notice spiders busily spinning their webs; see the intricate patterns they create. Wildlife can make you smile and encourage your sense of wonder.

COLOURS OF JOY

When you are out and about, look around: what colours do you see? Take in the hues of nature, the blue sky and white and grey clouds. If there are trees nearby see their green or russet leaves. Taking time to notice and appreciate the colours of nature is a quick and pleasant way to be more mindful.

If you have a garden, tune in to all your senses as you mow the lawn, dig the soil and tidy the flowerbeds – or just sit peacefully and enjoy your surroundings.

If you don't have a garden, go to a park and notice the shrubs and flowers, their colours, their texture and any scent they may have. Notice the pebbles and grass. Really look at them and enjoy their special uniqueness. Pay attention to nature's beauty, it is all around us.

The **mind** in its natural state can be compared to the **sky**, covered by layers of **cloud** which hide its true **nature**.

Kalu Rinpoche

MINDFULNESS, THE ROOT OF HAPPINESS.

Joseph Goldstein

TRY SOMETHING NEW

It is easy to be mindful when you attempt to do something you have never done before. The way we behave when we are learning – moving slowly, taking care over our actions and considering each choice – is how we behave when we are being mindful. So to enjoy more moments of mindfulness take up a new hobby or activity. It doesn't matter what it is: it could be learning Spanish or scuba diving, or going to a dancing class.

Learning something new will also benefit your life in other ways outside of your mindfulness practice! Learning stimulates the mind and introduces new ideas into our lives. If you engage in a social hobby you may even welcome new friends into your life. As you master your new skill you may have to work harder to remain mindful, but you will also feel positive emotions such as confidence and a sense of achievement.

Living in the present moment creates the experience of eternity.

Deepak Chopra

TODAY IS THE FIRST DAY OF THE REST OF YOUR LIFE.

Charles Dederich

Nature does not hurry, yet everything is accomplished.

Lao Tzu

BRING YOURSELF BACK TO THE PRESENT

Three times a day, for one minute or so, simply stop whatever it is that you're doing and take notice of the feelings and thoughts in your mind. Are multiple things whizzing through your head or are you concentrating on the present? If you realize that you are distracted, guide your attention back to the task in hand. Becoming more familiar with your mind's habitual patterns can help you to work with them much more skilfully.

Be where you are,
otherwise you will
miss your life.

Buddhist proverb

The **only** true thing is what's in front of you right **now**.

Ramona Ausubel

MINDFUL MEDITATION

Meditation increases present moment mindfulness. That in turn is what makes us happier and healthier. It's no wonder that it is popular because it is so powerful. Try meditative breathing. Focus on your breath and really understand that you exist in this moment. Breathe deeply. See each breath filling your entire body. When you focus on just your breathing, your mind escapes past events and future anxieties.

You don't need to carve out a large amount of time in order to effectively meditate. Like mindfulness, it can be absorbed into your everyday routines. When you finish one task don't immediately go into the next. Stop and breathe meditatively for several minutes (set a timer if you are short on time or at work so that you do not overrun). You will bring calm into even the busiest days.

The basic root of
happiness lies
in our minds; outer
circumstances
are nothing more
than adverse or
favourable.

Matthieu Ricard

LIFE IS A DANCE. MINDFULNESS IS WITNESSING THAT DANCE.

Amit Ray

THERE'S NO NEED TO BE PERFECT

Immerse yourself in activities for the enjoyment they bring you, rather than with the goal of trying to achieve perfection. Dance because you love to move to music, not just because you are determined to improve your footwork; bake bread because you enjoy the comforting feeling of kneading dough and the aroma of the loaf while it is baking. Focus on the task in hand and enjoy it for the pleasure you feel when doing it. Imposing additional demands on yourself will detract from the joy of the activity.

Good is good enough. No one can achieve perfection in every part of life so pick and choose those areas where you feel content to be "just right". The results will be emotionally liberating.

AN OASIS OF CALM

Turn your home into a harmonious sanctuary by making it as calm and peaceful as it can possibly be. You could hang wind chimes at a window or in a corner of a room to help attract and invigorate your home's natural energy. You could also add a vase of fresh flowers or a thriving green plant and some perfumed candles. Each soothing element can be something to focus your mindfulness practice on – note the gentle sound of the wind chime or the beautiful bloom of flowers as you move around your house.

If we shall take the
good we find, asking
no questions, we shall
have heaping measures.

Ralph Waldo Emerson

NATURE'S BEAUTY

All flowers are beautiful, but how often do you look at them without really seeing them properly? The very next time you see a flower, stop and look closer. Consider it carefully. Is it all one colour, or a combination of several? Look at its petals; are they large or small? Inhale the fragrance. Mindful practice can help you better appreciate beautiful objects and gifts of nature.

An awake heart is like
a sky that pours light.

Ḥāfeẓ

With every
experience,
you alone are painting
your own canvas,
thought by **thought**,
choice by choice.

Oprah Winfrey

LIFE GIVES YOU PLENTY OF TIME TO DO WHATEVER YOU WANT TO DO IF YOU STAY IN THE PRESENT MOMENT.

Deepak Chopra

MOVE THAT BODY

Be aware and stay mindful of how your body reacts throughout the day. If you notice it feels tense in certain areas, perform movements that help to restore and refresh you. For example, if your shoulders are tense, to release them stand up and shake out your arms.

Move as much as possible throughout the day, especially if your job or lifestyle is sedentary. If you are stuck behind a desk most of the time, stand up and move around for a few minutes every hour or so. You could add extra movement on your work commute by standing instead of sitting on the bus or train, walking to the next bus stop on from your usual one or parking further away from the office in the car park. Mindful movement helps boost your mood and your mental health.

Every **morning**
I do 10 minutes of
mindfulness… and I use
that in **competition**
and **everyday** life.

Tom Daley

ALL YOU NEED
IS DEEP WITHIN
YOU, WAITING
TO UNFOLD AND
REVEAL ITSELF.

Eileen Caddy

SWITCH OFF GADGETS

Nowadays it seems we are constantly bombarded with a non-stop stream of information from mobiles, computers and television. It can be overwhelming. Once in a while, turn off devices, put away any gadgets and give yourself some time off from the lights and noise. Sit quietly and calmly. Be aware of your thoughts.

Become comfortable with the peace and quiet. Try it first of all for 30 minutes. Then do it for a morning on your day off. Go for a walk, try a new recipe, do some embroidery, enjoying the feeling of peace it brings. You will feel so calm afterward and it will allow you to tap into the part of yourself that is often disconnected from the world around you.

IF YOU AREN'T IN THE MOMENT, YOU ARE EITHER LOOKING FORWARD TO UNCERTAINTY, OR BACK TO PAIN AND REGRET.

Jim Carrey

Nothing ever gets anywhere. The **earth** keeps turning round and gets **nowhere**. The moment is the only thing that **counts**.

Jean Cocteau

HUMDRUM TASKS?
ENJOY THEM!

Don't rush through your daily chores.
Think about what you are doing and
become absorbed in the process.

Be completely present in everything
you do and savour every detail. For
example, when you are washing up,
notice every bubble the washing-up
liquid makes, enjoy the sensation of
warm water and take pride in the clean,
fresh dishes when you have finished.
You will feel a sense of satisfaction.

Put your **ear** down
close to your **soul**
and **listen** hard.

Anne Sexton

Every time we become
aware of a thought,
as opposed to being
lost in a thought,
we experience that
opening of the mind.

Joseph Goldstein

DITCH THE CLUTTER

A tidy home goes a long way to promoting the feeling of well-being. Decluttering is great as it helps you let go of the past and renews energy. A great deal of clutter in our homes could be eliminated by being more mindful in the present. Mindfulness makes us aware of our surroundings. Removing old items helps us to stop living in the past and start living in the present. Don't overwhelm yourself by trying to clear every room in one go; be realistic, take it calmly and clear one room or area at a time. The past is behind you, let it go. Afterward, you'll feel amazing!

Your **vision** will become clear only when you look into your **heart**. Who looks outside, **dreams**. Who looks inside, **awakens**.

Carl Jung

NEVER BE AFRAID TO SIT AWHILE AND THINK.

Lorraine Hansberry

MIX IT UP

It's all too easy to find that you are stuck in a rut. This can happen by standing in the same place on the platform every morning waiting for your train, having the same thing to eat for lunch every day or always taking the same route to work.

Consciously think about adding variety to your daily routine – whether it means sitting on the upper deck of the bus for a different view of your surroundings, or taking up a new hobby in your lunch break. Make a point of taking a day out just for you and do something that you like, or go and visit a new place.

Varying routine tasks means we refresh our experience and stops boredom setting in. The same old routine can drag us down if we don't reform it occasionally.

Meditation practice isn't about trying to throw ourselves away or become something better. It's about **befriending** who we are already.

Pema Chödrön

True solitude is a din
of birdsong, seething
leaves, whirling
colours, or a clamour
of tracks in the snow.

Edward Hoagland

EMBRACE THE ELEMENTS

Do you try to avoid going out when the weather is bad? Does the rain or wind make you want to stay indoors? Next time you hear yourself complain about the cold or the wet, change your mindset and look for the opportunity in the bad weather. For instance, if you haven't seen the latest film you might say, "It's a great day to venture out to the cinema!"

A walk in the rain can add another dimension to your mindful behaviour thanks to a heightened sense of smell and sound. Look at how the wind blows through the tree branches and hear the leaves rustling. Nature is wonderful; take time to notice and appreciate it. The elements, whatever form they take, refresh and revitalize us.

Having a wider heart
and mind is more
important than having
a larger house.

Venerable Cheng Yen

RELEASE YOUR INNER CHILD

Every once in a while, pretend to be a child again. Do you remember how curious you were then? Mindfulness is seeing things with fresh eyes. Bring back those childlike moments and find a new way to behave mindfully. Children see magic in everyday things: raindrops glistening on leaves, stars twinkling in the sky, the slow but sure progress of a snail making its way across the garden. Look around and start seeing the world through a child's eyes. It will brighten up your day!

TAKE TIME TO THINK

If you fill your whole day with activities, you will find yourself rushing from one thing to the next without stopping to think about what you are doing. Doing less means you can fulfil those activities more mindfully, more completely and with more concentration. Maybe you think you are so busy that it is not possible to do less? You can. Assess what is important and let go of what isn't.

Mindfulness is like entering a darkened room and turning on the lights of perception.

David Pollak

The wise man is
a happy child.

Arnaud Desjardins

DO NOT FEAR MISTAKES. THERE ARE NONE.

Miles Davis

MANDALA MAGIC

Mandalas are geometric designs with circular patterns. They may be employed for focusing the attention of practitioners, as a spiritual guidance tool, for establishing a sacred space or as an aid to meditation. They have been used for thousands of years in Buddhist and Hindu traditions. Creating a mandala can be a great way to begin to express your thoughts and feelings.

The process of creating a mandala lets you tap into your creativity and can help you become more aware of your inner thoughts, so you can make positive changes through building clarity and consciousness.

Choose a design that appeals to you and let your mind be absorbed by the patterns and colours. Focusing on the shapes and patterns brings our senses into the present moment while colouring in a mandala is an excellent mindfulness technique to relieve stress.

SIT. BE STILL.
AND LISTEN.

Rumi

Don't let
yesterday use
up too much
of **today**.

Cherokee proverb

BE GOOD TO YOURSELF

Perhaps you are well on the way to practising mindfulness daily now, but you are still slightly concerned that you cannot sustain it all the time. Sometimes you may feel you are too busy to practise, or that when you do you can't stop your mind from wandering. Do not feel annoyed at yourself at these times; forgive yourself instead. Self-compassion will enable you to try again. You will get there in the end; do not doubt yourself.

Don't let fear or insecurity stop you from trying new things. Believe in yourself. Do what you love.

Stacy London

STAY GROUNDED

When you find yourself standing around waiting, let's say for a bus, bring your awareness to your feet and their connection to the ground. This helps you to gain a sense of equilibrium and balance. Stand with your shoulders relaxed, back straight and pelvis tucked under. Breathe deeply, be mindful and enjoy the wait.

Leading a busy life means pressure is never far away. This means we often yearn for the minutes to pass more quickly during the times that we spend doing "nothing" such as standing on a train platform or in a coffee shop queue. It makes more sense at these times to employ mindfulness techniques instead of wishing precious time away.

It is very **simple** to be **happy**, but it is very difficult to be **simple**.

Rabindranath Tagore

BREATHE AND LET BE.

Jon Kabat-Zinn

THE GIFT THAT'S FREE

Mindfulness needn't cost anything because you can get started without any equipment or training. All you need is the willingness to devote some time and space to access your mindfulness skills every day. However, if you feel you'd like to take your mindfulness practice to the next level, consider going to a local class or invest in one-to-one tuition. Learning in a group has the benefit of an atmosphere of community and friendship.

If you prefer to learn in your own home, you could try an online course or buy a mindfulness CD to guide you. Whichever method you choose to embark on your mindful journey, always remember, practice makes perfect.

Let your life lightly
dance on the edges
of Time like dew
on the tip of a leaf.

Rabindranath Tagore

IF YOU WANT
TO CONQUER
THE ANXIETY OF
LIFE, LIVE IN THE
MOMENT, LIVE
IN THE BREATH.

Amit Ray

RISE AND SHINE

The benefits of getting up earlier in the morning to spend some focused time on yourself pays off. Really, it does! Try to get up at least half an hour before you usually do and luxuriate in being able to complete your morning routine mindfully and purposefully. Those extra minutes give you time to think, to focus on what you want – perhaps to do some yoga or stretching exercises. It will help you sustain a feeling of calm throughout the day.

Time is a created thing.
To say "I don't have
time", is like saying
"I don't want to".

Lao Tzu

TOO MUCH INFORMATION

We are probably exposed to as much information in one day as our ancestors received in a lifetime. Our brains are overstimulated. A cluttered mind is a stressed mind. Cancel subscriptions for magazines you may not read and unsubscribe from catalogues and junk mail. Free your mind up, make space for peace and notice how much calmer you feel.

How much of your life
do you spend looking
forward to being
somewhere else?

Matthew Flickstein

REMEMBER TO BREATHE!

It's true, sometimes we forget to breathe! Deep breathing is good for you. During busy days, pause for a moment and try a mindful breathing routine. Place one hand on your chest, the other on your stomach. Inhale through your nose. Keep your mouth closed. When you exhale, open your mouth and relax your shoulders and upper body muscles.

Close your mouth and inhale slowly through your nose, letting your stomach rise up and out. When you've inhaled as much air as you can comfortably, stop. Open your mouth and exhale, gently pulling in your stomach. Do this two or three times, or as many times as you need to feel calmer.

Life is denied by lack of attention, whether it be to cleaning windows or trying to write a masterpiece.

Nadia Boulanger

Whatever the present moment contains, accept it as if you had chosen it.

Eckhart Tolle

THE TIME TO BE HAPPY IS NOW, AND THE PLACE TO BE HAPPY IS HERE.

Robert G. Ingersoll

CONCLUSION

I hope you have enjoyed reading *The Little Book of Mindfulness*. As you continue with your mindfulness sessions, you will see the beneficial effect they have on your mental clarity and well-being.

I wish you well on your mindfulness journey, and if reading this book has helped improve your life, why not give it to others as a gift? It may help them, too.

Seize the moment and give your best to today.

Life is lived now, not tomorrow.

If you're interested in finding out
more about our books, find us on
Facebook at Summersdale Publishers
and follow us on Twitter
at @Summersdale.

www.summersdale.com